D1498932

Louis Weber, CEO
Publications International, Ltd.
7373 North Cicero Avenue
Lincolnwood, Illinois 60712

www.pilbooks.com

Manufactured in China.

8 7 6 5 4 3 2 1

ISBN: 1-4127-4047-9

baby talk

WELCOME TO OUR WORLD!

Written by Steve Heinrich

new seasons™

Every climb to the top
starts at the bare bottom.

You said you wanted
to see a clean bowl
by the end of breakfast.

Don't ask me how
ocean water is better
than bathtub water.
It just is.

What I'm trying to say here
is babies need more kisses.

You've got it backwards.
Grandpa John looks like me.

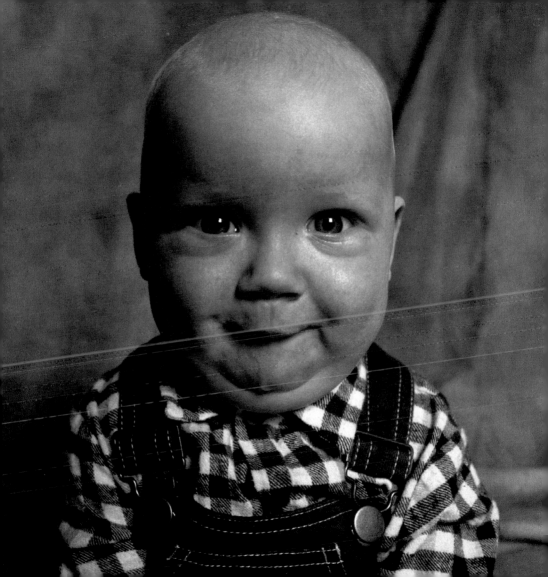

I know, I know.

Five seconds ago I was crying

because I wasn't on the horse.

Maybe if I stick my finger
in there I won't have
to take a bath . . .

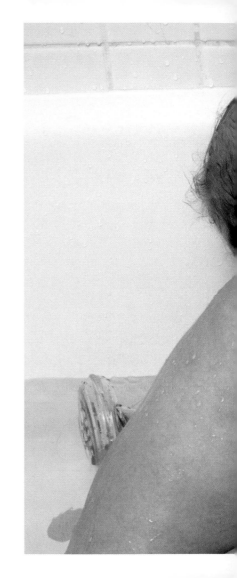

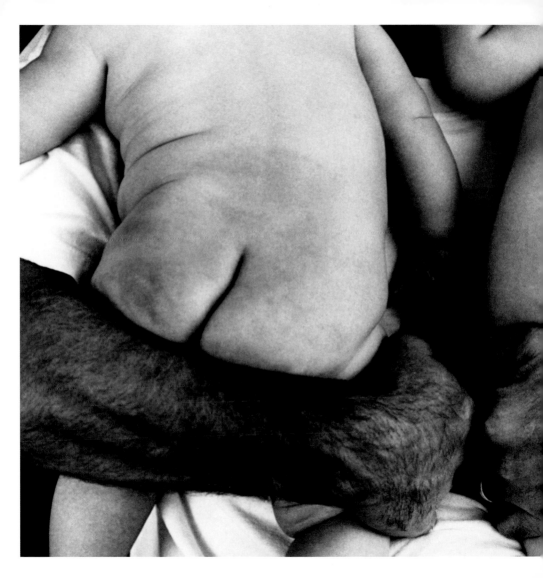

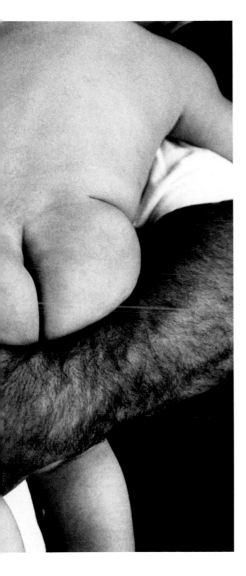

Let's just be a
couple of bums today.

17

Eat strained carrots?
Ha! That's a good one!

But I don't feel like a big boy.

The difference between naked and nekked?
Naked is when you don't have clothes on.
Nekked is when you don't have clothes on,
and you're up to something.

Oh, no!

Mine must have fallen off!

Attention! Attention!
I need attention!

Please can I do something I shouldn't?

You're right!
I am picking up something.
And I'll probably
put it in my mouth.

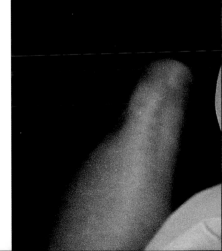

If all babies
were the same,
yours couldn't
be the best.

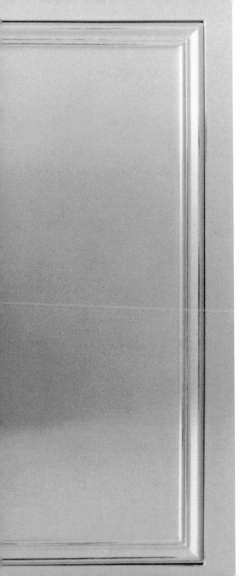

And *so* what if I am
delivered before the crib?

And you wonder why we grow up
and just have to have
what all the other kids are wearing.

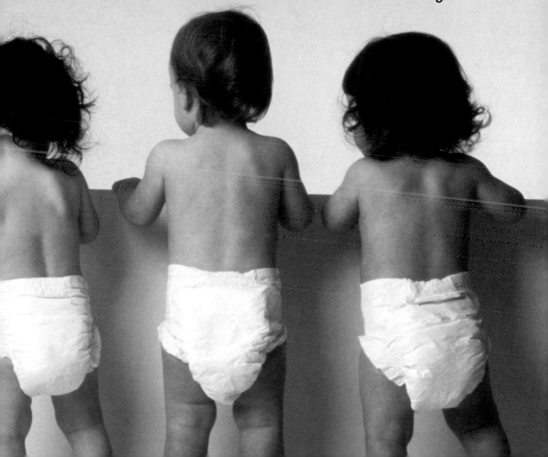

How's that newspaper
thing workin'
out for ya?

39

Please hand me that *so* I can
throw it on the floor again.

I'll be going back
to this look when I'm 14,
so get used to it.

I agree.

Babies in black just ain't natural.

I think it's a good idea
to leave your bedroom door
open for me in case . . .
WHOA! What are you two doing in here?

Yep, time for a change.

Mmmm . . .
peanut butter, right?

It goes like this:
I look real cute, and you
give me whatever I want.

100% puddleproof.

Hey!
I'm turning into
a prune here!

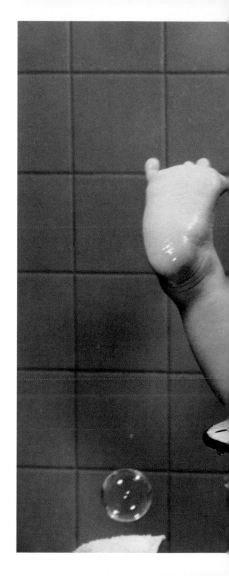

Whatchutalkinbout, Mama?

What are you going to do
with those scissors?

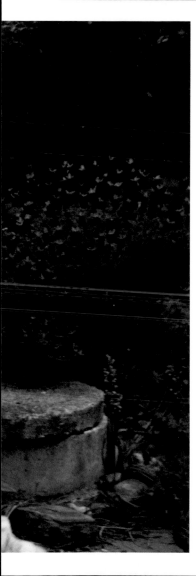

Okay, now,
my turn to play with it.

I have no words,
so my only language
is volume.

I will NOT sleep
when you want me to.

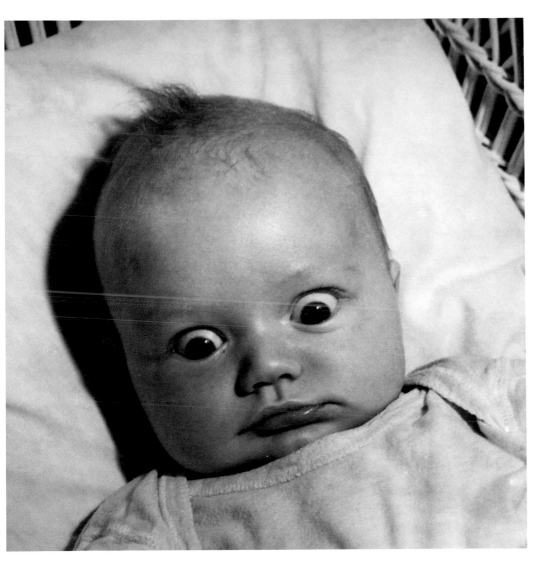

Yeah, this is the one
you'll be reading to me
every night for the next two years.

This feels *so* good I could
. . . and I did!

You give me wings.